# YOUR KNOWLEDGE HAS VALUE

**Bibliographic information published by the German National Library:**

The German National Library lists this publication in the National Bibliography; detailed bibliographic data are available on the Internet at http://dnb.dnb.de .

**Imprint:**

Copyright © 2015 GRIN Verlag, Open Publishing GmbH
Print and binding: Books on Demand GmbH, Norderstedt Germany
ISBN: 9783668379664

**This book at GRIN:**

http://www.grin.com/en/e-book/351099/ethnic-groups-in-indonesia-the-javanese

Elisabeth Schmid

**Aus der Reihe: e-fellows.net stipendiaten-wissen**

e-fellows.net (Hrsg.)

Band 2241

# Ethnic Groups in Indonesia. The Javanese

GRIN Publishing

**GRIN - Your knowledge has value**

Since its foundation in 1998, GRIN has specialized in publishing academic texts by students, college teachers and other academics as e-book and printed book. The website www.grin.com is an ideal platform for presenting term papers, final papers, scientific essays, dissertations and specialist books.

**Visit us on the internet:**

http://www.grin.com/

http://www.facebook.com/grincom

http://www.twitter.com/grin_com

# JAVANESE

Cross Culture – Ethnic Groups in Indonesia

8. NOVEMBER 2015

ELISABETH SCHMID

Bachelor C30

# Table of Contents

# JAVANESE

## Introduction

There are over 300 ethnic groups and more than 700 living languages in Indonesia. Some of these ethnic groups are totally different from each other. On the other hand we can find some ethnic groups that are very similar too. With 95.2 million people, Javanese build the largest ethnic group of Indonesia. I am very interested Javanese, because I have been to Yogyakarta and was able to experience Javanese culture. That's why I choose this ethnic group.

1 Javanese people

## Data and Facts

### Population

In 2011 there were 95.217 Million Javanese, which was 40.22% of the Indonesian population. Today there must be over 100 Million. This number makes clear, that Javanese are the biggest ethnic group of Indonesia.

### Main regions

Javanese are native to Java Island, but they are predominantly located to the central and eastern part of Java. The main region where we can find them are Bengkulu, East Java, East Kalimantan, Central Java, Jambi, Lampung, North Sumatra, Riau, South Sumatra and Yogyakarta.

## Sub-ethnic groups

There are many sub-group. For example the Mataram, Cirebonese, Osing, Tenggerese, Boyanese, Samin, Naganese, Banyumasan.[1]

## Language

Javanese people speak Javanese. It is the mother language to more than 98 million people.[2] It belongs to the Austronesian language family. There are also many groups of Javanese dialects. The three main dialects of 'Modern Javanese' are 'Central Javanese', 'Eastern Javanese' and 'Western Javanese'. There is a dialect change continuing from Banten, (western Java) to Banyuwangi (eastern corner of the island).

Javanese is written with Javanese script, (a descendant of the Brahmi script of India), Arabo-Javanese script, Arabic script (modified for Javanese) and Latin script.

A speaker of Javanese must adapt his "speech level" according to the status of the person addressed. There are basically two "speech levels": *nikko* and *kromo*.

*Nikko* is the language in which a person thinks. It is only allowed to use nikko with people of equal status. Close friends or people, whom one knows intimately, and with social inferiors.

*Kromo* is spoken to older people, people of higher status, and those whose status is not yet known by the speaker. Many of the most basic sentences differ markedly at the two levels. In nikko, "Where [are you] coming from?" is *Soko ngendi.* In kromo, it is *Saking pundi.* Mastering kromo is an acquired skill.

In addition to polite speech, proper respect requires appropriate body language: bowing and slow, graceful movements.

## History of Javanese People

The Austronesian ancestors of the Javanese arrived perhaps as early as 3000 BC from the Kalimantan coast. Over the centuries, different

---

[1] http://sp2010.bps.go.id/files/ebook/kewarganegaraan%20penduduk%20indonesia/index.html
[2] *Kewarganegaraan, Suku Bangsa, Agama dan Bahasa Sehari-hari Penduduk Indonesia - Hasil Sensus Penduduk 2010.* Badan Pusat Statistik. 2011. *ISBN 978-979-064-417-5*

native Javanese states appeared. Most were coalitions of regional lords.

In the 15th century AD., Java's north coast ports fell under the influence of Muslim Malacca, and under the rule of the descendants of non-Javanese Muslim merchants.

In 1830s the Dutch government took control of Java. In the 19th century a population explosion turned 3 million Javanese into 28 million. The Javanese took the lead in the Islamic, communist and nationalist movements that challenged colonialism from early in the twentieth century.[3]

2 20th century, Dutch colonialization

## Religion

Animism was the first religion of Java.[4] In the northern coast area of Java, Javanese people came in contact with Islam for the first time. This took part in the Majapahit period, when Javanese traded with various states like Perlak and Samudra Pasai (today it is called Aceh). Today most of Javanese (93%) are Muslims[5].

There are just a few Javanese following Christianity, even less Buddhism and Hinduism, which can be also found in the Javanese community.

Kebatinan, also called Kewjen, is a Javanese religious tradition, consisting of a combination of animistic, Hindu-Buddhist, and Islamic beliefs and practices. It is about the search for the inner self but at the core is the concept of the peace of mind, connection with the universe, and with an Almighty God. It addresses ethical and spiritual values as inspired by Javanese tradition.

---

[3] http://www.everyculture.com/wc/Germany-to-Jamaica/Javanese.html
[4] Muhaimin 2006, p. 2.
[5] Geertz, Clifford (1976). *The religion of Java*. University of Chicago Press. ISBN 978-0-226-28510-8

## Major Holidays

The first day (beginning at sunset) of the Islamic year, called *Sur,* is regarded as a special day. People stay up all night. They watch processions such as the *kirab pusaka* (parading of the royal heirlooms) in the town of Solo. Many meditate on mountains or beaches.

The birthday of Muhammad *(Mulud)* is celebrated in Yogya and Solo by holding the Sekaten fair the week preceding the date.

Ancient *gamelans* (a type of orchestra) are played at the festival. On the holiday itself, there is a procession involving three or more sticky-rice "mountains" (symbolizing male, female, and baby)

## Ceremonies

Many of the Javanese ceremonies have their roots in Kebatinan. Also they can be different from one community to the other. In the following text I will explain a few of them. [6]

Grebeg Maulud is a traditional ceremony held by the royal court of Keraton Surakarta and Jogjakarta, to celebrate the birth of Muhammad, the Islam's holy messenger. The ceremony starts with prayers in the grand mosques, a parade and a carnival of the people.

The Javanese wedding wedding ceremonies are different from each other and depend on the social standing of the couple. Popular variations includes Surakartan, Jogjakarta, Paes Kesatrian, and Paes Ageng. The wedding rituals will include *Siraman, Midodareni*, Peningsetan, Ijab (for Muslims) or wedding sacrament (for Christians). [7]

*3 Javanese wedding*

---

[6] http://www.javaans.net/index.html
[7] http://www.jagadkejawen.com/index.php?option=com_content&view=article&id=7&Itemid=7&lang=en

On *Siraman* the bride and groom to be are showered at their respective homes, by families and close friends. Prayers are also given hoping for a good tide.

*Midodareni* is the night before the Javanese wedding. The bride-to-be has her last dinner with her family, female friends are also invited. Traditional cuisine and prayers are given. Later, the groom's family will also come, bringing Peningsets (offerings to the bride family to seal the tomorrows wedding) in which the bride-to-be is hidden in her room. Only the female relatives of the groom can visit the bride-to-be.

*Naloni Mitoni* is celebrated, of a women is pregnant for her first time, in the seventh month of pregnancy family and close friends are invited. The mother to-be is covered with seven layers of batik, which means hope for a good delivery and a healthy child. There is also traditional food and prayers.

*Khitan* is an import tradition for boys towards adulthood. The boy has to be between 6 and 12 years old. There is a goat that is sacrificed. Then there will be a *slametan*, which is a ceremony with rayers to hope for good tidings, and also a *wayang kulit* (shadow puppet) performance.

*Nyekar* is hold before the month of Ramadhan, family members visit the graves of their loved ones, praying for their wellbeing.

## Javanese personality

Javanese avoid confrontation at all costs. They react even to disturbing news with a resigned smile and soft words. They never give a direct refusal to any request, but will try to give hints.

Age is an important determinant of social status in Java. The younger person defers to the older person, in language and in attitude, even when the age difference is negligible. It often happens that Western companies send their best and brightest person, who happens to be young, to negotiate or work with an Indonesian company. The managers at that Indonesian company will immediately feel a little insulted that somebody more "authoritative" was not sent to deal with them. [8]

---

[8] http://livinginindonesia.info/item/the-javanese

# Family

The family and social life plays an important role for the Javanese. A traditional Javanese could never imagine to be separated from the life of his family.

The respect of the parents and ancestors is essential. The father as the head of family and mother as the backbone. There is a Javanese saying: *'mikul duwur, mendem jero'*. In English it is "carry on shoulders highly, bury deeply", which means always honor the parents and ancestors, remember the good things they have done, forget the bad ones.[9]

# Culture

## Music

Like in the whole world, also Javanese music has many different types and directions. But the main element of traditional music in Java is **Gamelan.** There is Gamelan in whole Indonesia, but it is slightly different from culture to culture.

The full gamelan orchestra is an important part of traditional rituals, festivities, and theater. It consists of bronze gongs, keyed metallophones, drums, a flute, a rebab fiddle, and a celempung zither. It also includes male and female vocalists. The music includes hundreds of compositions in various forms.[10]

*4 Gamelan orchestra*

## Dance

Compared to the dances of other cultures in Indonesia, the Javanese reflection too. Dance contains slow movements and graceful poses. It is kind of meditations and self- Traditional dance emphasizes control of the body. Movements are very slow and graceful. Dance is also seen as kind of a meditation and self-reflection.

---

[9] http://www.joglosemar.co.id/family.html
[10] http://www.seasite.niu.edu/indonesian/budaya_bangsa/Gamelan/Main_Page/main_page.htm

The most revered dances are the *bedoyo* and *srimpi*. Male dancing includes the *tari topeng* in which solo performers portray fairytale characters.[11]

5 Javanese dance

## Batik

Batik is a traditional technique of dyeing fabric. The basic process is simple. It consists of permeating an area of fabric with hot wax so that the wax resists the penetration of dye.

To finish one piece of batic art usually takes between one or two weeks. Some very ornate pieces can take up to one month.

In old times, a women had to finish one Sarong with Batik technique before she could get married. The process of dying is a training of patient. With finishing her first sarong a women proofed to be ready for marriage.

6 Batic art

---

[11] http://www.joglosemar.co.id/trad_dance.html

## Cuisine

Javanese cuisine is sweeter than in other Indonesian areas. Most of the time, Javanese meals contain ingredients like rice, stir-fried vegetables, dried salted fish, tahu (tofu), tempeh (a bar of fermented soybeans), krupuk (fish or shrimp crackers), and sambel (chili sauce).

### Favorite meals

Following there are some favorite dishes described in detail:

*Sate*: grilled meat

*Soto*: Javanese soup with tomato, egg and some vegetables. A famous form is soto ayam (soup with chicken)

*Gorengan*: assorted fritters such as tempeh, tofu, yam, sweet potato, cassava, and chopped vegetables

*Urap sayur*: Vegetables in spiced grated coconut dressing

*Lotek*: Almost identical to Gado-gado (vegetable salad with peanut sauce), but sweeter.

*Gado-gado*: salad of partially boiled vegetables eaten with a peanut sauce

*Sayur lodeh:* vegetable and coconut milk stew

*Pergedel:* fat potato fritters


The folling dishes have a Chinese origin, but are very popular as well:

*Bakso:* meatball soup

*Bakmi:* fried noodles

*Cap cay:* stir-fried meat and vegetables

## Traditional specialties

There are also some very traditional meals. For example **Gudeg**. It is a traditional food from Yogyakarta and Central Java which is made from young Nangka (jack fruit) boiled for several hours with palm sugar, and coconut milk.[12]

*7 Gudek*

**Tumpeng** is rice, served in the shape of a conical volcano. Most of the times the rice is colored yellow with turmeric. It is served at special events like bithdays and other ceremonies. *Tumpeng* is served alongside fried chicken, boiled egg, vegetables, and goat meat on a round plate made from bamboo called *besek*.

*8 Tumpeng*

## Conclusion

Even though there are many similarities with other Indonesian ethnic groups, Javanese have a very unique culture. We can see this especially in the food culture. Also the Javanese character itself is very unique and different from, for example Balinese people, which are open-minded and open-hearted. Also religious background is very peerless. A visit to Java is a life experience.

[12] *Tempat Makan Favorit di 6 Kota.* AgroMedia. 2008. p. 136. ISBN 978-979-006166-8.ISBN 979-006-166-8.

# List of References

1. http://sp2010.bps.go.id/file/ebook/kewarganegaraan%20penduduk %20indonesia/index.htmls - E-Books Kewaraganegaraan Suku Bangsa Agama Dan Bahasa Sehari-Hari Penduduk Indonesia

2. Kewarganegaraan, Suku Bangsa, Agama dan Bahasa Sehari-hari Penduduk Indonesia - Hasil Sensus Penduduk 2010. *Badan Pusat Statistik. 2011.* ISBN 978-979-064-417-5

3. http://www.everyculture.com/wc/Germany-to-Jamaica/Javanese.html

4. Muhaimin 2006, p. 2.

5. Geertz, Clifford (1976). The religion of Java. University of Chicago Press. ISBN 978-0-226-28510-8

6. http://www.javaans.net/index.html

7. http://www.jagadkejawen.com

8. http://livinginindonesia.info/item/the-javanese

9. http://www.joglosemar.co.id/family.html

10. http://www.seasite.niu.edu/indonesian/budaya_bangsa/Gam elan/Main_Page/main_page.htm

11. http://www.joglosemar.co.id/trad_dance.html

12. Tempat Makan Favorit di 6 Kota. AgroMedia. 2008. p. 136. ISBN 978-979-006166-8.ISBN 979-006-166-8.

# List of Figures

# YOUR KNOWLEDGE HAS VALUE

- We will publish your bachelor's and master's thesis, essays and papers

- Your own eBook and book - sold worldwide in all relevant shops

- Earn money with each sale

Upload your text at www.GRIN.com and publish for free